On the Breathing Train

Caprice Leach

BookLeaf Publishing

On the Breathing Train © 2023 Caprice Leach

All rights reserved.

No part of this publication may be reproduced, stored in a retrieval system, or transmitted, in any form or by any means, electronic, mechanical, photocopying, recording or otherwise, without the prior written permission of the presenters.

Caprice Leach asserts the moral right to be identified as author of this work.

Presentation by *BookLeaf Publishing*

Web: www.bookleafpub.com

E-mail: info@bookleafpub.com

ISBN: 9789358368840

First edition 2023

DEDICATION

For K. L.

ACKNOWLEDGEMENT

Acknowledging E. M., S. D., C. V., and J. R. R.

PREFACE

"On the Breathing Train" is Caprice Marie Leach's first released collection of poems. It combines works from several years worth of poetry, along with poems written specifically for this book. These poems follow a chronological progression, beginning in July 2022 and finishing through May 2023. Some individuals of the collection were written in New York or Norway, while the majority were written in San Diego, California.

romance for cockroaches

lime-stench hangs
shapes
to the station walls while
women wallet-whine and
ensnare and twine
their hair and wind
their eyeballs twist
the sockets
their
fingers tear
the air
splinter-thick
in
thin-strips
we purchase tickets with
a dictionary
in reverse
letter-flipped
every word
we watch a
cockroach wedding
we catch our first bird
the dress always remembers
the first clothing-line
yellow

never stays
white
she was not just his wife
she was his bride
the lights attack
to kill
pigeon-eyes will
swell
in the sewer
flesh for newborn flies
we slit the throat
of the subway
the subway never dies

fault-line

the weight of a gaze
one can carry
with them
whipping sandstorms
scratching
at the glass
i lie witness to a sinkhole
as i am waiting on streetlights
thinking (even here)
you have to fall into a landslide
to know that it's there and
i hate
to feel the eyes (even here)
i hate
that i can't tell
why i feel them (even here) when
spilled over me
five years ago
molten hardened
capped itself
and those
shards are larval
ripping lava
dripping my lip
in gold antenna

it's times like these
mitas nights
that i am glad
i smashed
both my car's headlights
the place
where blossoms crossed my face
removed eyesight
those hands erased
the touch-blind i
could have said no,
but didn't and
finally crushed is
that place and
those flowers are underfoot-traced
i never before could know
to hold
myself a waterfall
falling still
but slow…
slowly

instar

blue in color
the moths of butterfly brother
die
in the frozen summer
frost cocooning
wings
ballooning
in all
off-places
stuck-crease ailments
hail in
fountains and
2 more than you could
count in
1 scrape of flower-face
cold summer
caught them all

1 quake

then 2 by 2
they
fall

in the pink room

alarmed and enamored
the wind-blow
hammered
the doorframe
catching
a pearl-string of conversation
a day
only tornado
could tell you his name
purple-scrape the mountain brain
now i'm afraid
he only bird-bones his sentences
traces pencils in
pen-ink
erases stray lines
a death-rattle in his chest
he tries to drink
the air
he tries another record
the needle drops
but the music stops
all of the tops
of traffic signs
cut off
the earth

runs into
the unanchored sun
and all the people
scream
at once

he tries another record
he tries to touch her hair

dancers

there are so many things
i wish my heart could hear
those small spaces in which
soul transcends his
brain-coil fixtures
when
the skull lends its
bone-hood
and the night tends to
scissor
its way into the sky
with the
calming-crack
of an ice-head
the hammer-handle
steady-pounds itself
viscera-deep into
pavement-beat
and the kitchen bell screams
the nightwork navy
(as it usually does)
while i sit in my thoughts to
barricade the door shut
then
with rust on my tongue

sing slowly
to the drip of
moon
hanging lowest tonight

the power of cadence
the intelligence
of nightfall

the poem with the girl and the vegan restaurant

with lacquer monarch
tangled lobes sag
seven pink ring fingers
tip-touch in paisley graze and pale
and mauve
and hair holds lazy ribbon

the face may be pretty
with makeup
polished neck pearl
bobbing eve's apple
flicking lever-speed up and guided slowly
lower
by blue-eye layered laughter
leather
and around seventy short lashes

with plenty of
space   between
    each   other

tacky glue

the woman who
became her house
let her near-blond
perm-soiled
tambour-coil curls
wreath their ring
to the roof
let her
spools
salmon-thrash
the drawers where
dolls used to sing
to the hard-wood floors
sewed the room
shut
with thread-strings
one thousand loops
it seemed the
thin white things could
swing a weightless
rigid scarecrow fright
to the
bifold door-arms
meanline-stiff
cast-set

fold them tight
by militia
tiny toy locks
diaper pins
capped-pens
with pocket clips
plastic green
needles
the walls were
pink-hand paint held but
their plaster strength
out-played
the sprinkler-rain
and
acres away
she paced the place
chalk-dry toes had
danced
tried to stand
knee-less
tried
to press
flowers to the ground
ironed time-frowns
from her daughter's
golden
wedding dress
she could still scrape
an apple core clean

wearing clear-coat
pretend
the circle slices left
could
glasses-lens her cataracts
lend them back
to blue
she stencil-cut the sky
cloud-stamped the scene
rolled up the rug
until it was her tongue
she chewed and swallowed
his chair
her ears grew square
to imitate a fireplace
only soot
no flames
crooked-hand to foot
her back became
the backyard
she body-curled a baseboard
her throat took the chimney
her cry took the clock-chime
she buried one blue eye
and iris grew
yellow-rose while
windows replaced her
lips and nose
every stitch

a surgeon
clipped to her skin
took the wind
they traced black
against the birch-wood
her knotted knuckles
branch-suffered
through storms
her teeth stretched
seven feet
they agreed
to grow a fence each
her diamond ring
went flying
landed
between
landscaped legs
her last eye
lit the porch-glow
regurgitated driveway
belly-plump garage
she popped a straw
in her mouth
she sucked
a sidewalk out
bruise-massaged
her shoulders
and
threw them out

to color the street
peeled her nails off
glued together
they were glass
for a slide-fast door
she tossed
the trimmings
she made them
her moon
her lungs breathed
alive
the living room

on the breathing train

wormed out from
the picture frames
your tongue could taste the soil
it
could flower-trumpet to ant-hills
you told your legs to
run it's a race
pickup the pace
they were glued
in place
picked your nose
in class and
everybody laughed
you were fairy-winged in a
backyard
white lattice fingers
your papa's deaf
he only hears
about three
words
a day
you double-tip the yellow-cab
in
the city who kills his stars
you lay braces

to the crooked mile
for a
moon-smile
to chew
you could fill a room with what she knew
you could fill a room
you could feel the
track-work flowers bloom
you could not lucky-strike
a lung
tell the man on your left
you like the red
seats
the train,
it breathes
no weed-rows will make
a garden
start in 3, 2, 1
then
the scream of a gun
the holes in his nose
catch
the smoke
it turns his teeth
green
anais-stars monger fear
from the windows
you push your thumb through
the petal

of a rose
you paint
your name
on the breathing train

a disparity of spoons

i try to eat my rice raw
in the kitchen
i sometimes use
try to
make myself soup
but the dirty spoons
cry their
unclean eyes away
i try to chew
my tongue at night
tooth-bite the trees
tear a shape
bleed their bark
a disparity of spoons
hears me
after dark
i get
hungry
once a year
i drink
clear stew
from a bowl
and the sink
with the swan-neck
swallows me whole

so thinly strewn
my body folds
i never
wash the spoons
i watch them mold

the redthroated bishop

the redthroated bishop
careening through the bruise stroke of pews
makes its way to the door
extends a hand
touches sulfur with shock
breaks grounds with racing
frantic prayer

the redthroated bishop is whole
or so it thinks
it is bound by transparent ropes
often encouraging
the infected robes
stitched to its body
to billow windless

dramatic,
is the redthroated bishop

you may find it staring
hollow eyes
grandmother stare

you might just view it
grainy and drying

absent of skin

is the redthroated bishop

canthion

the upside-down eye
could walk the ceiling
like the floor
gloss over
dead
bedrock solid
in a twin bed
as a second set
(its self-same)
could remain
alive
box-made for
skull and brain
the other eye
could number-name
count the amount
of house-street
one-way
or worse
be the first to
force the mouth
to say
words
it could
twitch-play

erase
lash-brush
the last place
it touched
living eye
might open-face
a firework
it may
tear-trace
a flame

86th

locked into contemplation of streetlights
a woman compliments me
the most beautiful i've seen
wanting her body or
wanting to love her
or something
like that
i glance at   the space
where her left hand should be and it's
barely   even   left there

i pass a man
next
with paint-eye bending
a left-empty lid white and red and he   gets
arrested

some moths mimic butterflies
i don't   know why they do that
i should know why they do that

the old-wise seem
too near the creeps
the red-bleacher leg-lookers
in the Times Square streets and i can only stare

key-locking
them eye-wise when
granite-torn grates
against metal bench-face placed   will get
me   nowhere
it's from   up there
i wonder if
i should give   myself
to the city
i wonder if
the city

                        is

already mine
this sea i swear this
mottled-scream this ripping torrent
it takes all that's left they all
watch as it does
watch as it swallows us whole
watch   the full-flood the
sky-scrape the tear-torn
   they watch it all

1-0-2 stories tall
   and finally i fall
from the 86th floor

evil mcdonalds

Subway sandwich smells
tacked onto publicly caked chlorine vests
sopping with the
collective urination of the condominium
streak
my brain
around 2012.	The year plastic became
evil,
and so did McDonald's.
Your grandparents– yes, the fat ones
They would take you out on lavish invitation.
summoned, fiercely, to the ball.
"Oh, we must go! We must! For, it's the king's wish!"
so of course go we did,
through the squeaky gate,
off of matted Antelope carpet floors.
A sloppy, sticky web of diabetes and ovarian cancer
twisted since the 50's and with two kids–
a boy and a girl and a Nathan, 'whatever Nathan was!'
You'd remark–
then right on back to
Peggy Lee's Fever over the

crumbly Denny's speaker.
A green shirt at Dairy Queen for the next week.
Maybe that's why we got so fat,
and why my brother has worked
longer than me
to keep the weight off.
My body wants to eat in an unnatural way.
In a way like,
I wake up and
I get hungry, then
around the time the sun hits the sky's meridian,
I hunger again,
then wolflike, at night–
'moonlight
I think that's what forms that pattern on the carpet,
with black leaves mixing too',
That small brown man would say.
Staying up late that Friday with Grandpa on the burgundy couch,
one of the longest couches I ever saw.
When I want to eat I want
Three Meals a Day and Food Groups and
Sonic waitresses on skates in the Chevy BelAir
after school, out later than we should be
with dad.
But McDonald's…
Time melts in a Big Mac.
I could be telling you about the Scarlet Ibis

the week before the renovation,
when there was still
a Jimmy Neutron game that preceded the show
for my brother and I to gawk at,
little asses out
for any old homeless man
to canestab– or worse.
But with you   it was different.
You didn't care about that, and you'd been worn
out long ago,
over 30 years worn.
And you must have been tired,
I mean who isn't?
You couldn't remember my friend's names
in a red booth
no matter how many times I mentioned them.
Carbonation brain rot from   Diet Coke but
never, ever,   Pepsi.
Fluid dementia–
Anyway
there was a year
it was supposed to snow
in Sacramento.
Do you remember how excited you got? I was
too afraid of that Grinch blow up decoration
your neighbors had to
memorize the tiny houses you had
out on the mantle.
Ask me, I could not tell you a single one.

I could maybe name the cars.
What was your obsess with San Francisco and those
Painted Lady houses?
There are earthquakes in San Francisco. Don't go, you'll get hurt.
'I couldn't live there anyway, so far from my grandchildren?'
I don't think you ever knew
the true person that was your grandchild.
You took care to know the chosen things,
I play the clarinet.
My birthday is in April.
It has to have been 6 years now,
since the wave-washed girl screamed "Granny!"
at the ground
and I just couldn't cry.
That was the first time my grades slipped.
I try not to overstate but–
At any rate.
You didn't watch me graduate.
You would have wanted my hair long.
I wore it long
for you.
And I'm growing it out again
I don't think that my anorexia
would allow me inside another McDonalds for a Mac Jr,
and my wit will no sooner allow me to watch

politicians fool themselves on that television or
see my cardiac patient of a grandfather choke
out a laugh of agreement at some
conservative policy.
I wouldn't go.
Not even to pretend to be a boy on the
playground,
bubbled up between the glass of some
fast-food after-work   distraction
"Birds take their wings for granted, but so do the
retired."
If I had an identical twin, I'd be jealous of her,
My own beauty idolized and shared but mine
nonetheless.
So then I think carefully
of your strawberry haired doppelganger of a
sister and I
realize that she must have felt that way towards
you,
when you two were girls.
I remember my cousin wrote her name
on your kitchen table, and when you died,
it went to her and her
stuffy,
UC Davis student,
game-board enthusiast
of a boyfriend.
Maybe after death we return to it. That thing we
used to be.

I like when Grandma perms her hair. It smells
warm.
We usually didn't go to Taco Bell, but
there was this man there,
just outside the door,
twitching and
foaming and
turning
blue.
I think that you protected me and
took me inside to order.
The man had no legs. I learned   people were
scary.
And I didn't like Taco Bell in 2012.
Too many shapes and contrast colors
in the paintings on the
maleficent purple walls.
The place was unbalanced and the crackheads,
perched like
pirate parrots
at the
doors
surly weren't an invitation to my eyes.
I can't believe
our second lunches
were 2 hours at most.
When we were with you,
it felt like ages and eternity.
I think I chose moments carefully

to think of in these times
when missing you is familiar to me and
welcome,
like the numb-cold tips of my fingers.
Seeing your tiny face through the tunnel of a
straw and
sighing, reminding myself that
iced tea is almost here, about to try your
favorite:
an Arnald Palmer.
Still.
Anything is better than McDonald's.
There's even one in China! Or even on the
Moon! The Moon!
No.

I wouldn't touch a Bic Mac if it would bring you
back.
I don't think I could outlive the
thousand island tears.

the tired buffet

unmethodically
nautically
disorganized
brackish water could
baptize his ship
instead of champagne
he could finger-tip
touch a flame
and never
face the burn
they watched him fall
eight times
naked
to the nines
numbers were evil
only words
spoke to people
he could tear up
the grass
hear it rip
through his hands
sip hourglass sand
and
smooth the grooves
of his teeth

if you
flip his crown
upside down
the head of the king
will bleed
the shepard will eat his sheep
and the
flightless monarch will
tell his kitchen only
to feed his
sleeping queen
the king
wing-beats he
does not eat
he builds
the church of the birds
they fly him
off the side

the sound the sun makes

i dissected
my glasses
piled the lenses
clothes-line dry
then
fountain-penny threw them
imagined that i
could eat my eyes
he could describe in
one
syringe-shot why
the jay had dyed his feathers
blue
he could pick you up
and carry you
arriving
at the airport
i cremate myself alive
ash-fly the plane-wing
i near-sight
the sky

inertia

the blind man had been writing his
racist, rape-ish,
Amsterdam novel;
naval, audile
with a cadence for annoyance, an
unnoticed hand-wobble, and
letters that seemed less esteemed to the touch
of his work-fingers
he
knew he couldn't read
braille in his gloves…
when he tripped (caneless)
over a crate that day,
spilling his brains,
one for each page,
they all clogged the drains as passers-by
pinched
paperpuddledflood and arranged
their wads of wetness
coffeebloodstained
around the crack in his skull
and the scold's bridle door-frame
a bumped up sign
for the willfully blind:

"here lies a story
its author has died"

japanese mock orange

the tiny girl,
she used to be,
had toothpick legs, finishing in
mismatch, too-large feet
one: tatter-ripped slipper
one: purple highheel
lifting these heavy things
over pinecones and craneflies
gripping trim-nail holes through the
olive-stain, finger-paint
brown bags of paper she carried
small girl assigned fates to the
dead-seemed
the little things
and red stones and rustless metal
and rolling bugs
in violent capture
and headless toys with imagined thought
and even she
pretended to be
a boy sometimes with scrotal shirtless tyrant; she
an ant upon her own boat-leaf
holding
an eyeless
african iris

tight inside this
throat with the voice
with the
croak she never
learned quite to like and
stealing from her remaindered brother
of two years younger
his only letters of different colors
from the left portion of the whirlpool fridge
a cut-grass, subcutaneous, shortcut
that mi-nute maggot must have loved thursdays,
might have had
her own thesaurus made,
and could have always
looked cool
in a mailman's sun-shades

the loud chewing

the canyon is transient
i think of the way that i could rest here
in its breast
for almost eternity
and then i hear it—

the loud chewing

it starts as a
pop
the twist of tongue
swiping teeth
hitching, sliding, suction, the squelch
the insistence of grinding gnaw
the sluice of saliva
deluge of spit and noodle
slurp   pop
lick
and then again—
slurp
pop
lick
squelch   as teeth click
i think i've had enough now
the canyon becomes her swollen lip

jaw gaping, squishing shut
putty-noodles/leaking orthodontics
pieces plastered/enamel braces
tightly wound/snapping masseter
over and over and over and over
slurp pop lick slurp pop lick
lick pop lick lick   click
and then again— over and over
i'd throw myself into her canyon mouth
before i ever told her
to stop the chewing
the impossible
mashed up
pounding   squeeze–
of the loud chewing

… pop

answering-name

on brewster mill circle
where the mock-orange stench was
angry with sun-heat
and the sidewalk chalk
blue
sank deeper
to make the cracks
black
i stepped over each one
by two
my very first wedding
was my first spiral staircase
my first
stone entryway
i hid in a hedge
carried sand in my hands
and drank a sip of champagne
spelled my name
till my cheeks turned
red
sometimes
you look in the mirror
and tip your head to the side
i would try
to see myself

with my eyes
closed
i let rabbits return my library books
sat inside of my shoes
slid and slipped
down the laces
i skinned my knee
and it
dripped sap instead of blood
but i was
worried
what i would say next at the
funeral for bugs
that i didn't even notice
i had fallen
off my feet
the tongue of the talker
never sleeps
and neither do i
on rainy nights
tossing shadow puppets
across the sheets
dancing wind
through a family of beans
turning the curtains
green
pumpkin-gut halloweens
dye flowers down
in vinegar

it
stains my Easter dress
my grandpa had
floss in his pocket
my brother sat
on a newborn snail
i cried
for nine nights
i claimed olives
upon my feet
commanded the wind
with a tree
cats run from vacuum cleaners
the same
cats will always die
sell a summer
in lemonade
paste it in marker-shapes
i wish i could kill
mathematics and numbers
i sometimes wish
i could kill my mother
i almost fell off
of a horse
i slash the screen
of the sliding door
black widows nests
burgundy cabinet flesh
light bulbs bursted

an owl-less brown fence
we visit their gravestones
a little less
every year
i hate the cut-down tree
at nanna's house
but she loves the sunroom here

big fish (from "the god of the birds")

we could count
if we wanted
– our backs to the sandstone
each scale of the air
doorpass through the
crack, concrete-wise, in the sky
i tell you
i could taste you in the sea
if i try
so you jumped me
up on your back
and threw me in
with that
green blush
memorized by your eyes
etching the oceanlines further
into the stone
and parallel to the
fishbone cross-section
of the stars

- for J. R. R.